REINVENTING YOUR BUSINESS WORKBOOK
PANDEMIC EDITION

ISBN: 978-1-7366505-0-9 (Paperback)

REINVENTING YOUR BUSINESS WORKBOOK: PANDEMIC EDITION
How to move forward when you don't know what will happen next.
By Eric L. Byrd

First Edition
Cover design by Eric L. Byrd

Printed in the United States of America
MLP Technologies, LLC | 202 Church Street SE Suite 100 | Leesburg, Virginia 20175

Visit the book website at: www.reinventingyourbusiness.net

CONTENTS

Table of Contents

What Do I Do Now?

At the moment it's November 2020. We're in the eighth month of the 2020 COVID-19 pandemic. I've been helping small business owners since March and it's always the same question. What can I do? The question is normal, the situation is not. Far from it..

The pandemic has created a historic level of uncertainty and turmoil, especially for small businesses. Revenue and activity is down. Customers are hesitant. Owners are struggling.

Back in April I had an thought. As I was listening to "experts" talk about how companies would have to change their models and pivot their business I got worried. Not because they were wrong. I was worried because I work with small buisinesses every day and I know that a lot of them wouldn't know how to do those things. The planning tools and management methods most use are not designed for this. Plans were for multiple years, not weeks. Many didn't have any kinid of written plan at all. They live month to month, customer to customer.

Nor was normal disaster planning enough. Usually disasters are a big disruption for a short time. Then assistance helps rebuild back to what you had before. This was not going to unfold that way. All the epidemiological models said it would drag out for months or more.

As I pondered the problem, I began to see a way to help. I realized we needed very, short term plans instead. A process you could repeat over and over, as long as needed. Under normal circumstancees this is too inefficient for a stable business. It is more like what a startup does.d. In this crisis it might be just the ticket. You're not thinking long term. You're thinking survival. The focus is keeping your head above water until the flood waters recede and you can stand up.

How to plan when you don't know what will happen next week.

When things change you must change too. Things are fluctuating unpredictably in quick succession. We're locked down. We're open.. We're partially open, but withrestrictions. Then the restrictions change, then change back. Now we may shut down again.

Everyone wants things to go back to normal. That won't happen for many more months, even after a vaccine is released. How can you take action now? This process will show you. It can help avoid the traps of paralysis (doing nothing), avoidance (doing nothing new), or panic activity (frantically trying to do everything). None will help you move forward.

This workbook will guide you through a process that can help. It won't be easy. There is no magic answer. However, you can find creative solutions and sustain through the crisis.

This is a step-by-step process to help your business survive the turmoil until things stabilize. Once they do you can begin to recover profitability.

I wrote this book as a way to help you make it. Good luck and God speed!

Think Like a Startup

To make it through the crisis I'm asking you to adopt a startup mindset. Startups must regularly question assumptions and adjust what they do based on what they learn. Brand new companies face uncertainty daily. They don't know if their idea is valid, or not at the beginning. They adapt and improve so they can survive.

The strive to understand what their customer think is valuable first and foremost. it's the core of everything in a business. What do they want? How do they want to get it? What will they pay? How will they use it? Where are they? Who are they? This is the heartbeat of your business.

No value, no sale. No sale, no company.

When facing change or turmoil, you have to go back to basics. Every business faces change eventually. Customer's change. Technology changes. If you don't know why your customers want what they want, you may miss the signs and become irrelevant. Your ability to stay valuable in your customer's eyes is the key to your success every day. It's doubly true now.

What do customers really want?

Knowing what customers actually see as valuable is the key to this entire process. It's what your core assumptions are based around. Know the 'why' of your customers and you can create something they will find value. They will buy value. Even during a pandemic.

When change happens we have to re-check what customers find valuable. They may no longer be what they were before. In 2020 so many things shifted for everyone that many industries were severely disrupted. Things don't work the way they did before. People don't do things they did before. That might hurt your business. If you can adapt, it could help your business.

This happens normally for all businesses. It's usually just slow. In a crisis it happens much more quickly, so we feel it immediately. You must react more quickly with less certainty.

It's like being a startup all over again. Start by recognizing what you did before will not work now. During crisis your resources are often limited and customer behavior changes suddenly. Identify those changes, focus your resources and you can survive.

It's about quick, decisive action.

The business plan you had won't work, so you have to create a new one. Actually a bunch of them, in quick succession. This workbook lays out a way to help you shift and change to respond right now. You will create and execute plans in short bursts focused on what your customers find valuable right now. Not down the road, but today. Because you need them to buy something this week. Strap on your startup helmet and let's jump in.

YOUR GOAL: SURVIVE, SUSTAIN, AND RECOVER PROFITABILITY WHEN THINGS ARE MORE STABLE

If you're stuck or don't know what to do...
this workbook will help you start taking action.

If the challenges make you anxious or fearful...
this can help you breathe and sleep again.

If you are unsure or hesitant...
it will give you confidence to act boldly and with purpose.

If you are looking for hope and guidance...
it will help you find a positive direction again.

This workbook will guide you through the process step-by-step.

The exercises and questions are designed to make you think creatively. You'll evaluate your situation, come up with creative solutions to challenges, map them out as tasks, and then take action quickly to make things happen.

This is not a traditional business planning process, but it has many elements that may feel familiar. You will set short-term goals and work to achieve them. I'm asking you to put aside long term goals here. This is a rapid response methodology to help you figure out how to keep your business alive through a period of instability. You can come back to long term planning once things are more predictable and stable.

If you would like to see some other resources based on this process, or the source books and processes I baed it on, feel free to visit: www.reinventingyourbusiness.net.

Using the PACE Cycle

This workbook revolves around a process I created called the PACE cycle. It is the core of this very short term business planning methodology. It is simple, but powerful.

PACE is a repeating set of step by step exercises and activities so you can plan and act during a very short timeframe. Mostly you'll look at the next 30 or 60 days in your business.

During times of disaster or sudden change, deciding what to do next can be an overwhelming challenge. PACE provides a structure for decision making and action. It provides the ability to react and remain flexible.

In an emergency you must act fast. In crisis we tend to do the obvious things first. The thing you can see. Get out of the house. Call 911. Move to higher ground. Stay out of the water. You don't worry about the long term.

Priorities are different and in flux. You run into many unknowns. A disaster plan may help, but it assumes things will go back to normal relatively quickly. After a hurricane or tornado ends you rebuild. Maybe exactly what you had before the disaster.

What if the crisis doesn't end quickly? Like COVID in 2020. Then what do you do? This is one reason 2020 has been so hard. The disaster is ongoing, with no end in sight yet.

PACE addresses this problem by walking you through four steps of the process;

Pause, Assess, Create and Execute.

Each step contains exercises and activities to hel pyou develop and initiate an action plan for a very short period of time. Then PACE allows you to do it again, and again. As long as needed.

This workbook has all the instructions, exercises and shows forms you can use to learn the PACE process. The idea is that you can use it to face any turmoil and extended change with purpose and confidence. Now let's look at what you can expect from each section.

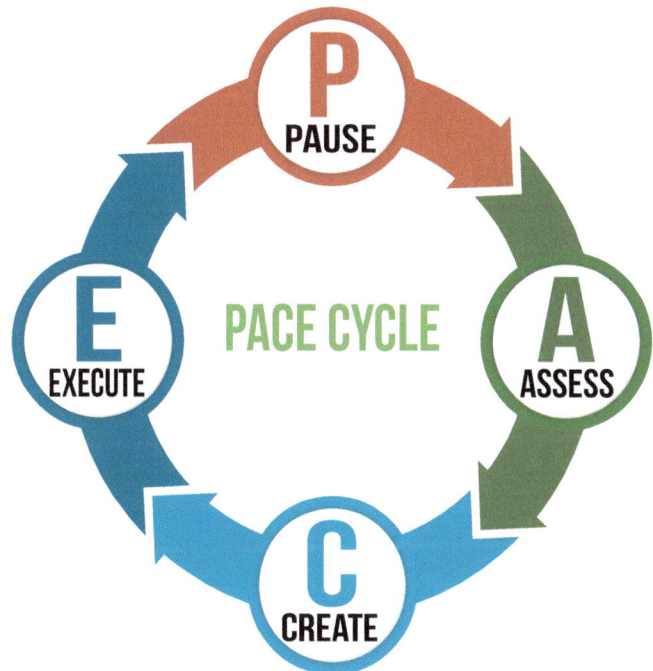

Here's How It Works

This workbook will show you how to get a handle on your current situation, guide you to set goals and make decisions about which actions you can take to move your business forward, and provide you a way to manage those actions during a very short period of time.

Since you can't do long term planning during a crisis, the system is designed to be used during times of uncertain and instability. The tools will help you focus on finding ways to take action quickly to respond to an immediate danger to your business.

To get you oriented, here is an overview the steps in the process and what each entails. That way you'll have an idea what to expect from the rest of the workbook.

PAUSE for Planning

You have to start somewhere and for PACE it's with a pause to reflect and roll up your sleeves. By taking a breathe to organize yourself and gather information, and a few folks to help, you will begin taking control of your situation. You'll be asked to pick a start date and pick a short time frame to focus on for the rest of the process.

ASSESS Your Situation

Having gathered yourself and a team, you'll take a hard, honest look at your current business situation. You'll evaluate your financial situation, your customer's behavior, your current activities and processes. You'll get a sense of how you feel about the business at this moment. This data will be written down for this cycle to help you organize the data. This puts the information at your fingertips and helps you use it to create a plan of action for the next month or two.

WHAT TO EXPECT

CREATE a Plan of Action

Once you take stock you can identify goals and tasks to help improve your situation. I'll show you simple ways to gather the information and use it to generate a list of things to focus on during the cycle. This gives you direction and confidence so you can focus resources and efforts where they can do the most good. It helps you be as proactive as you can given the situation you find yourself in now.

EXECUTE the Plan Using Agile

You'll jump into action using a project management process called a SPRINT. You'll identify tasks to work on every week. Each week you'll attempt to complete those tasks. Each task will help you move forward to drive revenue, control costs or nurture future business, as you see fit.

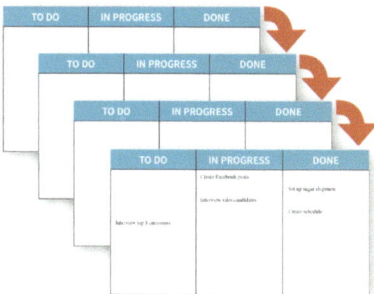

During each PACE cycle you'll do multiple SPRINTs, adjusting as you go to keep you on track and moving forward towards the goals you set.

The advantage of a SPRINT is that it keeps you focused and allows you to change direction if needed.

At the end you'll PAUSE again and do a review. You'll identify lessons learned, and note what future improvements to take forward.

Then you can start a new PACE cycle, if needed, and repeat the process. You can do that as often as needed.

STEP 1:
PAUSE FOR PLANNING

PAUSE and Get Ready

This is an opportunity to get your bearings. It's a short step, yet it is vitally important. Don't skip this. You're setting the stage for what follows. Take a moment to do three things:

1. Define the cycle length and start date.

PACE helps you focus on a short period of time. The first step is to choose the length of the cycle. I recommend 30 days the first time you go through the process. That will give you a chance to learn the process. Avoid looking too far down the road. That's one of the challenges we're addressing here, lack of information about the future. Record whether you are choosing a 30 or 60 day cycle. Once you're experienced you can use longer cycles.

2. Choose some people to advise and support you.

Next, identify your PACE team. They will be your support team for this cycle. Choose people you trust to give good, thoughtful advice, who will tell you the truth and know about your business. Some of them may also help you execute the plan, but that is not required. You might pick some of your management team, your accountant, banker, a primary vendor, a critical employee, or a business coach. Whoever you feel can help.

3. Gather information and documentation.

You will need information as you do the exercises and create your plan. Now is a good time to gather your primary business information so you have it handy. Any information about what has been happening lately can be useful. Finding those documents now will save time and help you keep your momentum once you begin answering questions with your PACE team. Data helps you make better decisions. Get yours ready.

Here are some things you might want to have as you start:
- *Basic business information (EIN, addresses, contact info, etc).*
- *Sales/Revenue reports for last 30 - 90 days.*
- *Expense Reports for last 30 - 90 days.*
- *Customer lists, vendor lists, suppliers, etc.*
- *Bank statements, account numbers and bank contacts.*
- *Invoices, payables accounts or other accounts due soon.*
- *Industry contacts, reports, websites, articles, etc.*
- *Operational manuals, procedures, employee list, etc.*
- *Website analytics or marketing reports for last 30 - 90 days.*
- *Social media, website, email and other account information.*

STARTING A NEW PACE CYCLE

Choose Your Cycle Length (30 or 60 days)		Cycle Start Date	

PICK YOUR PACE TEAM

Name, Organization		Position or Role	

Above is a form you can use for this exercise. If you have the capability, you can print it and fill it in by hand. You can also just draw your own on a sheet of paper, notebook, on a flip chart, or a whiteboard if you'd prefer. Then you can fill in the information for each cycle as you see fit.

Visit www.reinventingyourbusiness.net to see what on-line or downloadable tools as we develop them. They are not required but you may find them valuable. Full disclosure; supplemental tools may be at additional cost.

STEP 2:
ASSESS
YOUR SITUATION

ASSESS

In This Section...

You will evaluate where things stand at this point in time. I suggest you be as honest and candid as you can with your PACE team here. You're going to look at multiple areas of your business and it can be a little uncomfortable, especially if you don't like sharing information about your business with other people. It's important. It will help you figure out what comes next.

Take a look at six elements of your business.

There are six areas of your business to consider in this stage. Be prepared to take as much time as you need for this process, but no more. Try not to over analyze either. Your goal is to work quickly and move on to action. Getting too detailed can cause more confusion, not less.

This information will become the basis of your goal setting and decision making in the next stage of the process. Good data here makes for better decision making and opens up creativity.

Time to Complete: 1 to 2 Hours (average)

You should be able to do this exercise within a couple of hours if you have all the data and information at hand. It may take a bit longer the first time as you get used to the questions.

Here are the areas you'll be looking at specifically:

Financial Checkup

A quick look at what funds you have, what's coming in and what's going out this cycle.

FINANCIAL CHECKUP

ASSETS & REVENUE		LIABILITIES & EXPENSES	
Available Cash		Fixed Monthly Expenses	
Available Credit		Variable Expenses (this period)	
Monthly Sales (last 30-60 days)		Other Expenses (this period)	
Other Revenue (this period)		Liabilities Due (this period)	
Total $ Expected (this period)		Total $ Needed (this period)	

Customer Checkup

Answering the question "what are my customers doing and why"?

CUSTOMER CHECKUP

Describe your top 3 customer groups (name or short phrase)	How often are they buying?

What product/service is each group purchasing?	Why are they buying that now?

Key People and Partners

Who is going to be important to your business during this cycle?

KEY PEOPLE AND PARTNERS

Name, Organization	Position or Role

Activities Checkup

What are you spending your time on and what's different than before?

ACTIVITIES CHECKUP	
How are you delivering to clients now?	How are you keeping in touch with customers now?
What activities are you focusing on now?	What are the three biggest challenges you face?

SWOT Analysis

What might help you and what might trip you up this cycle?

STRENGTHS	WEAKNESSES
OPPORTUNITIES	THREATS

Your "Gut Check"

How are you feeling about the business going into this cycle?

BUSINESS "GUT CHECK"

How are you feeling about the business overall?
(Okay, concerned, worried, or panic)

Do you feel you can continue this business effort?
(Yes, probably, unsure, or no)

What has happened to sales over the last 60 days?
(Increase, steady, or decrease)

What is the general trend in business activity now?
(Better, steady, or worse)

Taking a hard look at where you are now.

Each exercise will be explained in more detail as you go through the workbook.

Looking at these areas will allow you to take stock of your resources. It will also give you a chance to identify the environment and what activities have been occupying your time. You may find some things to do better, or spot something to take advantage of you missed previously. This information will enable you to figure out what is most helpful, what's realistic and hopefully give you the data you need to brainstorm some new ways to approach your situation.

While you do this anallysis take advantage of the input from your PACE team to make sure you've gathered meaningful information. Their questions and feedback can be particularly helpful in getting outside your own habits and thought process. Share enough information with them that they can ask useful questions and understand what's really happening. They might notice patterns or trends that you don't see from your vantage point.

Specifically pay attention to why your customers are behaving the way they are at the moment. Remember, your business hinges on providing value they want to buy. You can get valuable insights from them as you move forward and make plans for bringing in more business.

Finding new and better ways to engage with customers and potential customers is often the most critical activity you can do. That especially true early on or when something changes.

ASSESS

Your Financial Situation

This will help you identify resources so you can set financial priorities for this cycle.

Assets & Revenue:

Available Cash: *How much cash does the business have? (Total of all sources and accounts)*

Available Credit: What *credit is available? (Include all available loans, lines and cards)*

Monthly Sales: *What do your sales look like right now? If you're not sure use the average for the last 60 days or how much you expect to sell this cycle as a forecast.*

Other Revenue: What *other revenue you expect this cycle, if any? Do you have Invoices coming due? Any past due receivables you can collect? Recurring revenue being autobilled?*

Total $ Expected: *Total of all the above sources to give you a Total Expected Assets figure for this cycle. This is what you will probably have to spend during this cycle.*

Liabilities & Expenses:

Fixed Monthly Expenses: *Add up any costs that don't change each month like rent, insurance, lease/loan payments, etc. These are the regular expenses you plan for each month.*

Variable Monthly Expenses: *Estimate totals for any costs that change each month like labor, utilities, fuel, supplies, etc. These are the regular expenses that aren't always the same amount.*

Other Expenses: *Are there any other expenses due during this period? Non-monthly bills due like quarterly insurance, dues, equipment payments, any seasonal costs? Include them here.*

Liabilities Due: *Do you have anything else you might need to pay for this period? Special loan terms ending? Any payables due not covered by the other categories? Add them up and put the amount here. Just to cover all the bases, if you have any.*

Total $ Needed: *Total all the liabilities for this cycle. This helps you understand fully what you are probably going to need to pay out for during this cycle.*

This section may be uncomfortable.

When you've added up all the positive and negative numbers it's possible that things won't look good at this point. It may be difficult to really see how bad things are right now. You still need to do this. Knowing the reality of your situation is the first step to changing it for the better. Taking this honest look at your finances will empower you. Now you know what you're facing.

It's better to know than not to know. Take a deep breath, then move on to the next assessment.

ASSESS

FINANCIAL CHECKUP

ASSETS & REVENUE		LIABILITIES & EXPENSES	
Available Cash		Fixed Monthly Expenses	
Available Credit		Variable Expenses (this period)	
Monthly Sales (last 30-60 days)		Other Expenses (this period)	
Other Revenue (this period)		Liabilities Due (this period)	
Total $ Expected (this period)		Total $ Needed (this period)	

Above is a form you can use for this exercise. If you have the capability, you can print it and fill it in by hand. You can also just draw your own on a sheet of paper, notebook, on a flip chart, or a whiteboard if you'd prefer. Then you can fill in the information for each cycle as you see fit.

Visit www.reinventingyourbusiness.net to see what on-line or downloadable tools as we develop them. They are not required but you may find them valuable. Full disclosure; supplemental tools may be at additional cost.

Current Customers

Your customers are the life blood of your business. Knowing what's going on with them is the key to brining in as much revenue as possible. This exercise asks you to focus on your top three customer groups. Not everyone will buy from you right now. Identify the customers who are most likely to have a positive impact on your business right now.

1. List your top 3 customer groups.

Who is buying already, or who do you think is most likely to buy, during this cycle? Define the group as you see fit using whatever description makes most sense to you (e.g.. new parents, bike shops, office employees working at home, existing members, 55yo trapeze artists, etc.).

2. Note how often they buy from you.

When do your best customers purchase? Is it "often", "regularly", or "not often" (or daily, weekly, monthly, etc.)? Something to indicate when you'll see revenue from them. It's a critical pattern.

3. Identify primary products/services.

What are those best customers buying, or are likely to buy, this cycle? Which product and or service is most in demand to them at the moment? It may be different than before. Stay aware of the trends.

4. WHY do you think they are buying?

This is super important. What is driving them to purchase those specific things at this time? Try to think from the customers perspective. What do THEY think it's valuable in the current situation? Being able to put yourself in your customer's shoes will help you separate your opinion from their reality and enable you to see more clearly what can bring in sales right now!

Why this step is so important.

It can't be repeated enough, understanding how your customer thinks is critical to your success. Their perception of value is everything. Knowing how they think helps you determine what to offer them **RIGHT NOW. That will drive sales**

If they normally purchase one thing, but now buy another you need to know. Use this in the next section to decide what actions can drive revenue or reduce costs. We want to base decisions on evidence and data, not just opinion. It reduces uncertainty and builds confidence. The better your evidence about why they act this way the better your decisions.

Be concise and specific.

There isn't a lot of room to write in each line on the form. That's on purpose. You don't want to get lost in minutia. Be brief and use few words. You're writing for you, not to impress anyone else. If it makes sense to you and you can use it to act, then it's good enough.

ASSESS

CUSTOMER CHECKUP

Describe your top 3 customer groups (name or short phrase)	How often are they buying?

What product/service is each group purchasing?	Why are they buying that _now_?

Above is a form you can use for this exercise. If you have the capability, you can print it and fill it in by hand. You can also just draw your own on a sheet of paper, notebook, on a flip chart, or a whiteboard if you'd prefer. Then you can fill in the information for each cycle as you see fit.

Visit www.reinventingyourbusiness.net to see what on-line or downloadable tools as we develop them. They are not required but you may find them valuable. Full disclosure; supplemental tools may be at additional cost.

ASSESS

How You Spend Time

Time is a resource we often forget about. Focusing priorities to make sure critical things get done is especially important when there is a crisis or you're faced with unusual circumstances.

1. How do you deliver to your customers?

Fulfillment is an important activity for any business. How are you doing it now? What is the process? Has anything changed? Are you using new delivery, shipping, pickup or other options? What are the most critical aspects of that process for your current conditions? It may be an area where other changes may help, or resources may be required in the plan.

2. How do you communicate right now?

How are you keeping in touch with customers? Are you using email, telephone, social media, snail mail, video calls, smoke signals, or carrier pigeon? What marketing, sales or advertising channels are active? Are you making sales calls (in or out bound)? Are you sending physical mailers with information about how to do business with you? Take a look to see what's effective and where you may be wasting time.

3. What activities are taking up your time?

What do you find yourself doing each day/week? Where are you focusing time and energy? Are you getting distracted? Where does your energy go? Are there new activities (like cleaning/sanitizing) that have been added? What takes up time? What takes thought and/or energy? This will help you notice time wasters and prioritize activitiees.

4. What is challenging you right now?

What's got you worried? Where do you feel stuck? What haven't you figured out how to do yet? What do you find yourself thinking about a lot? What do you think is going to be difficult this cycle? Heighten your awareness to notice whether you're sucked into urgent but not important things. This helps you create solid priorities in your goals and tasks.

Focus on important activities and any changes.

You're goal here is to identify anything you're doing that's important in deciding what to do next. Your action plan will be a set of goals and tasks. Staying focused on the highest priority tasks will help you make the best use of limited resources.

If you need to deliver to your clients in a different way, for example, note it. You'll identify all the details of that process later. Right now just mark that it's an important change to consider in your process. Making concious decisions about what you do makes resources stretch farther.

ASSESS

ACTIVITIES CHECKUP

How are you delivering to clients now?

How are you keeping in touch with customers now?

What activities are you focusing on now?

What are the three biggest challenges you face?

Above is a form you can use for this exercise. If you have the capability, you can print it and fill it in by hand. You can also just draw your own on a sheet of paper, notebook, on a flip chart, or a whiteboard if you'd prefer. Then you can fill in the information for each cycle as you see fit.

Visit www.reinventingyourbusiness.net to see what on-line or downloadable tools as we develop them. They are not required but you may find them valuable. Full disclosure; supplemental tools may be at additional cost.

Key People and Partners

Running a business is a team effort, even if you are a company of one or two people. There are others involved in what we do to consider. Identifying key partners keeps them on your radar as possible assets to leverage. You may come up with an idea in your plan where they can help you.

1. Make a list of those who are involved with your business.

Who is critical to the functioning of your busienss?It could be critical employees. It may be your key suppliers or vendors. It might be a partner, investor or service provider. These are people you depend on for products, serives, support or advice to keep operating? Who is positioned to get you critical information? Who provides feedback or useful input? Who will perform specific tasks or gets you key supplies for your operation? List them.

It might be someone in an industry organization. Maybe it's your business coach or your banker. It could be another group of business owners you lean on for moral support or a mentor you trust. Perhaps it's a client who can help you understand behavior or client needs. Any and all of these could be valid reasons to put someone on this key list.

2. List their role and/or relationship to you.

Who are they in their organization? How do they fit into your business? They may not work for you. They may work for a supplier or vendor. They may provide you a service you need right now. They could be an important team member that works for you.

We all need help to run our business.

Keep in mind, there are no wrong answers here. This is a list of resources you can reach out to for ideas, information or advice. You may depend on them for critical supplies or materials for what your company makes or delivers. Maybe they perform a specific and important function for you inside, or outside, your company. These are the folks who help you move things along.

Some businesses will need more key people inside the operation, some will need more partners outside. Your business may need both. Either is fine. Identifying these possible allies and supporters can also help you think more creatively when you're planning. It's a list of possible people to go to for help, support or ideas. It just might be that someone on this list will have the key information or a missing piece of the puzzle that helps you sustain through the crisis.

You may need to have conversations with them, if they're suppliers or vendors, about your plan so they keep the goods flowing. Discussing extended terms could make or break things if they're really tight one cycle. Your partner's success is also linked to yours. Keeping them in the loop on what you're doing to remain viable can make them feel more comfortable helping too.

ASSESS

KEY PEOPLE AND PARTNERS

Name, Organization	Position or Role

Above is a form you can use for this exercise. If you have the capability, you can print it and fill it in by hand. You can also just draw your own on a sheet of paper, notebook, on a flip chart, or a whiteboard if you'd prefer. Then you can fill in the information for each cycle as you see fit.

Visit www.reinventingyourbusiness.net to see what on-line or downloadable tools as we develop them. They are not required but you may find them valuable. Full disclosure; supplemental tools may be at additional cost.

ASSESS

Do a SWOT Analysis

SWOT is a strategic tool that looks at different factors in and surrounding your business. Doing this exercise can help you flag problems or spot an advantage that can help you susstain.

SWOT looks at two internal factors, *Strengths and Weaknesses* as well as two external factors, *Opportunities and Threats*. Two you control, two you do not. You need to be aware of all of them to make the best decisions you can about possible actions to face change.

When considering each think about your situation and the environment for the specific cycle period you've chosen. Keep your answers focused to THAT timeframe. No generic answers. That keeps the answers relevant and focused to the current situation.

Strengths:

Write down any positive, internal, attributes of your business. What do you do well? Resources, people, knowledge, skills, process, relationships, patents or technology that can help right now? Are you known for something specific? It could help.

Weaknesses:

List any negative, *internal, attributes of your business. What do you NOT do well? What resources, knowledge, skills, process, or relationships do you lack? What makes things difficult now? What might get in your way as you try and take action?*

Opportunities:

Jot down *positive, external things can you take advantage of right now? Be creative! Anything happening you can leverage? Any groups to partner with? Ideas you've heard about? You can use these opportunities to make your situation better!*

Threats:

Write down any negative, external things that could block, harm or impede your progress? *Are there new regulations? What economic conditions or lack of activity apply? How about competitors? Do customers need a change? Anything that might torpedo your efforts.*

Stay focused on the now during this exercise.

Again, don't drift into broac generic answers. Your winning personality might be a strength generically, but if it won't help you drive sales the next month it's not relevant or helpful. This is important because you will lean heavily on these answers during the next step of PACE.

Leverage your PACE team's input here! They can help you expand your perspective and see both positive and negative things you may miss. Take full advantage of their opinions.

ASSESS

SWOT ANALYSIS

STRENGTHS

WEAKNESSES

OPPORTUNITIES

THREATS

Above is a form you can use for this exercise. If you have the capability, you can print it and fill it in by hand. You can also just draw your own on a sheet of paper, notebook, on a flip chart, or a whiteboard if you'd prefer. Then you can fill in the information for each cycle as you see fit.

Visit www.reinventingyourbusiness.net to see what on-line or downloadable tools as we develop them. They are not required but you may find them valuable. Full disclosure; supplemental tools may be at additional cost.

How Are You Feeling?

Your mindset and emotions affect how you do business. It's helpful to be clear about them when you're facing crisis or change. There is no right answer to these questions. Just be honest. Remember, you're doing short term planning, so your attitude in the present is a factor. Intuition is an important part of a business owner's took lit. This helps you be more self-aware about your own positive or negative thoughts so they don't subconciously derail you.

1. How are you feeling overall?

Choose "okay, concerned, worried or panic". Don't over think it. What is your initial reaction? This doesn't mean you won't be able to figure it out, but if you don't acknowledge concern it can make it harder to be creative and brainstorm at the next step.

2. Can you realisticly keep this going?

Again, this isn't a finite answer. It doesn't mean you're giving up yet. It's just helping you check in on your ability to accept risk. Your mindset is critical regardless of whether you continue or decide to shut down or exit. Be honest with yourself. Going down with the ship is not the only option, and if it's time to consider an exit then admit it. If not, then forge ahead!

3. How are recent sales looking?

Is your revenue trending up, down, or staying the same at this point? It's easy to lose sight of the trends in the day to day grind. This gives you some big picture perspective.

4. What has your general activity been like?

What do you notice about general business activity? Are customers shopping more? Did you get fewer or the same number of inquiries over the last 30-60 days? Do you see more people out and about? Are vendors sharing more stories of positive activity or higher requests? This can help focus you on the future trend, which helps when you are planning what to do later.

Your feelings will change over time.

Your gut check will not be the same every cycle. It will fluctuate every week, every day, maybe even every hour depending on what's happening. Cut yourself some slack.

This is not designed as a hard 'measurement' of your abililty to continue your business. Let's also keep in mind that feeling unsure or pessimistic about your business isn't a failure. It may actually be quite normal and reasonable given the circumstances. Acknowledging it is an important part of the process. It keeps you present to the reality of your business. It will help you make productive decisions moving forward. Self-awareness is a good thing.

BUSINESS "GUT CHECK"

How are you feeling about the business overall?
(Okay, concerned, worried, or panic)

Do you feel you can continue this business effort?
(Yes, probably, unsure, or no)

What has happened to sales over the last 60 days?
(Increase, steady, or decrease)

What is the general trend in business activity now?
(Better, steady, or worse)

Above is a form you can use for this exercise. If you have the capability, you can print it and fill it in by hand. You can also just draw your own on a sheet of paper, notebook, on a flip chart, or a whiteboard if you'd prefer. Then you can fill in the information for each cycle as you see fit.

Visit www.reinventingyourbusiness.net to see what on-line or downloadable tools as we develop them. They are not required but you may find them valuable. Full disclosure; supplemental tools may be at additional cost.

STEP 3:
CREATE
AN ACTION PLAN

CREATE

In This Section...

In this stage you are going to identify actions in the form of goals and tasks for this cycle. You'll brainstorm goals that can improve your situation and identify the tasks that bring those goals into reality. You will also consider the every day operational tasks that you do to keep your business up and running so you can factor them into your action plan.

Your roadmap for what to do next.

A plan is simply a list of actions and guidelines for those action. Using your assessments as a baseline you can now think about what actions might make things better. They may be big changes or little tweaks. Your overall objective is to generate ideas to help sales, drive revenue and control costs. Cutting things may be difficult, but it might also be necessary. It may require some creativity and 'outside the box' thinking. Be sure to include your PACE team in this step. They may have practical and helpful ideas for things to try. Leverage their experience!

Time to Complete: 1 to 2 Hours (average)

This section can be exhilarating as you map out new things to try and set new goals for the coming weeks. Try not to get bogged down in the weeds. Don't lose sight of the short term focus. It's easy to be distracted thinking too far ahead. Keep it simple and immediate!

Here are the exercises you will be doing for this section:

New Ideas to Try this Cycle

What are some things you haven't done but could try this cycle?

NEW IDEAS TO TRY   DATE _____

What are two things you can try to decrease expenses in this period?

What are two things you can try to increase sales or revenue in this period?

What are two brand new things you can try during this period to improve things? (shifts)

CREATE

New Idea Evidence

Wat evidence makes you think those things will work at this stage of the game?

EVIDENCE FOR YOUR NEW IDEAS DATE

What evidence do you have that these things will decrease your expenses?

What evidence do you have that these things will increase sales or revenue?

What evidence do you have that these things will potentially improve your situation?

Goal Planning Sheet

What are some goals you could try and what are the tasks that are needed to achieve them?

GOAL PLANNING SHEET

PRIMARY GOAL	MILESTONES	TASKS

Goals for this Cycle

Which goals do you want to attempt right now to move things forward?

GOALS FOR THIS CYCLE — DATE _____

PRIMARY GOAL	PRIORITY	PURPOSE

Regular Operational Tasks

What are the regular, day-to-day tasks that need to be done?

REGULAR OPERATIONAL TASKS

DAILY	WEEKLY	MISC

Task Backlog This Cycle

What tasks are you going to need to do to operate and move towards completing your goals?

TASK BACKLOG THIS CYCLE DATE

TASK	PRIORITY	ASSIGNED	TASK	PRIORITY	ASSIGNED

Deciding what you want to do next.

Each exercise will be explained in more detail as you go through the workbook.

This step asks you to brainstorm and then make decisions about what you'll try over the next few weeks. Stay focused on sustaining and surviving first. Remember, it's all about increasing cashflow by deliverying more value to your customers in their current situation. Without that your position could worsen and you risk being able to sustain through the crisis period.

Include your PACE team in these exercises. They can help you see things you didn't notice or suggest things that may not occur to you. That's the value of multiple perpectives. It could make the all the difference to have just a little bit of progress in the next month or two.

As always, keep your customers at the core of your plans and activities whenever possible. They are the fuel. Figure out what they need or want and you can figure out how to get it to them.

This is where a narrow focus on your 'best' customers can help. They are usually the most willing to spend and most loyal to you. Which can help cash flow. They are also more likely to spread the word. Use that to your advantage. Think narrow and specific. It's easier to engage someone who already knows and get them to act than try to fight the noise and catch the attention of someone who doesn't know your value yet.

CREATE

New Ideas to Try

Whether you've been trying new things already or not, do your best to brainstorm a few new ideas. Use the assessment information to help spot trends and patterns that you might not have seen before. Give yourself permission to consider wild ideas too. It's your opportunity to put things on the table and look them over. It can be something you would never do normally that would help, even a little, under these conditions. You're not creating a long term plan here, you're looking for quick, decisive actions to try. Gather your PACE team and get creative.

1. What two things could decrease expenses?

Survival is still key, so keeping expenses as low as possible can help extend your lifespan. What are a couple of ways you can get lean, slim down or do without? Even one or two small ideas here can help your situation when times are rough.

2. What are two things that might increase revenue?

On the flip side, revenue is critical to keeping you viable. How can you pull in some more sales? Do you have outstanding receivables you can collect? A small project you can do that normally wouldn't be worth the time and effort? A niche customer need you can meet if you get creative? Try listing new ideas and see what your team comes up with to try.

3. What are two things that might be useful?

Time to think outside the box. Have an idea for a new product or service? Is there a twist on a service you haven't tried, but might get traction? What about changing a process to make things more efficient? Any way to get some attention? Can you leverage social media? Perhaps a "behind the scenes" story about your team could get some positive attention.

Looking into the Future

These six ideas can form the bsis of new goals to try this cycle. Even one really good idea can have a big impact on the next 30 to 60 days. Let your team be creative and go outside the normal lines. This is a chance to be bold. If the safe answers were working you wouldn't be in this position in the first place. Use this as a chance to stretch yourself and your business outside the comfort zone a little bit. What can you do that creates a reaction? How can you get things moving? It doesn't have to be perfect. Try to break things loose and get things moving.

CREATE

NEW IDEAS TO TRY

DATE

What are two things you can try to decrease expenses in this period?

What are two things you can try to increase sales or revenue in this period?

What are two brand new things you can try during this period to improve things? (shifts)

Above is a form you can use for this exercise. If you have the capability, you can print it and fill it in by hand. You can also just draw your own on a sheet of paper, notebook, on a flip chart, or a whiteboard if you'd prefer. Then you can fill in the information for each cycle as you see fit.

Visit www.reinventingyourbusiness.net to see what on-line or downloadable tools as we develop them. They are not required but you may find them valuable. Full disclosure; supplemental tools may be at additional cost.

Evidence for Your Ideas

The ideas you just listed came from somewhere. Take a few minutes to identify **WHY** you think they might work. This check makes sure you are thinking clearly and are using information to make decisions, instead of just grasping at anything in an effort to have anything to try.

Know why the ideas just might work.

Identifying supporting information or data about your idea helps give it credibility, for you and your team. You may not know why you had that idea, but that doesn't mean there isn't a reason.

You can use any information source that's relevant. Direct evidence from customers is always best, but there is no such thing as a bad source, if it's not just made up. Use sources that aren't just your own opinion. Hunches and feelings are useful tools in business, but they come from somewhere. What inspired you? Look at external sources for that hunch. It can give you a confidence boost too. Identifying those sources may also give you more information and spark other ideas too. Listing them makes it easier to go back to that well again later.

Possible sources of evidence:

Here are some suggestions for possible sources for information and evidence for your ideas. This is certainly not a complete list, but it may help as a good starting point.

- *Articles or industry reports sharing trends, industry sales data or stories about experiences from other businesses like yours (or in the same situation).*

- *Direct observations of customer behavior (are they calling more, asking for specific items, asking questions about a particular service, etc.). Make notes to refer to for ideas!*

- *Customers sharing their experiences, desires, frustrations, needs or situation. Even if it doesn't relate to your business it might help you understand how they're thinking.*

- *Social media posts, stories and/or comments sharing what people are doing, thinking, buying, experiencing, or talking about what they wish they had right now.*

- *Local economic development or business information about economic trends in your area.*

- *Political activity on regulations or economic assistance programs in your city, town or state.*

- *Comments or conversations with other business owners in your area or in your industry about their situation or experiences. Are they seeing the same things you're seeing?*

- *Information, requests and stories from conversations with vendors, suppliers or partners about the current level of business activity or how events are affecting them.*

EVIDENCE FOR YOUR NEW IDEAS   DATE

What evidence do you have that these things will decrease your expenses?

What evidence do you have that these things will increase sales or revenue?

What evidence do you have that these things will potentially improve your situation?

Above is a form you can use for this exercise. If you have the capability, you can print it and fill it in by hand. You can also just draw your own on a sheet of paper, notebook, on a flip chart, or a whiteboard if you'd prefer. Then you can fill in the information for each cycle as you see fit.

Visit www.reinventingyourbusiness.net to see what on-line or downloadable tools as we develop them. They are not required but you may find them valuable. Full disclosure; supplemental tools may be at additional cost.

Goal Planning

Time to turn your ideas into goals. If you want to launch a website to sell online, you need to define all the steps necessary first. Then those steps can be broken down into individual tasks. Those tasks are the things you 'do' during the execute step of PACE. Those individual actions move your company forward and help to improve your business situation..

I give an example of a simple sheet to map out the elements of the goals using a simple three part process. Since you may have more than one goal you may have more than one goal sheet. Your sheets may also need more milestones and tasks than I've included here, that's fine.

Each task that makes up your goal plan needs to be an action you can complete in one week or less. You'll understand why a bit later. We'll use a week as a measure in the next step of PACE.

It may turn out that you work on parts of one goal in one cycle, then come back to it in another cycle. How you execute will depend on your situation at that time. Don't worry about that right now. Once you create a goal sheet you will hold onto it for future reference, even if you don't work on it immediately. You can also create a goal sheet any time you think of a new goal.

You'll pick which goals and tasks to work on later. Right now focus on turning ideas into goals and goals into tasks. To start, identify a goal you'd like to try and do the following three things:

Set the Primary Goal to accomplish.

Write down the goal you'd like to achieve on the sheet. Primary goals can be large in scope, but that's not required. You can have a simple primary goal. For example, you goal could be to launch a new website with an e-commerce store. It could also be to hire a new cook.

Identify the sub-goals or milestones.

Are there segments to achieving that goal? List them. For the website you might have design the site, build the site, launch the site as three major milestones to the overall project.

List the tasks for each milestone.

Look at each milestone and determine the discreet steps needed to reach that specific milestone. These will become the tasks that you will manage later. In our website design goal the design milestone might have five discreet tasks. Keep in mind, tasks need to be able to be accomplished in a week or less. This will make executing in short bursts possible.

Now do the same steps for any goals you created from all of the new ideas you came up with in the previous step. Don't spend too much time on this, but be as acurate as possible. You can fine tune the details later, but getting as close as you can now will make things work more smoothly.

CREATE

GOAL PLANNING SHEET

PRIMARY GOAL	MILESTONES	TASKS

Above is a form you can use for this exercise. If you have the capability, you can print it and fill it in by hand. You can also just draw your own on a sheet of paper, notebook, on a flip chart, or a whiteboard if you'd prefer. Then you can fill in the information for each cycle as you see fit.

Visit www.reinventingyourbusiness.net to see what on-line or downloadable tools as we develop them. They are not required but you may find them valuable. Full disclosure; supplemental tools may be at additional cost.

Goals for This Cycle

Now is the time to decide what goals you want to work on this cycle. These are things that you feel will help you improve your situation. You may not reach the goal this cycle, but you've decided these are things that are important to work on now. This is an important time to consult with your PACE team to get their input.

Use the answers from your SWOT analysis to guide you here. Look for goals that can maximize your strengths, minimize your weaknesses, eliminate or minimize threats and take advantage of any opportunities you see in the present moment or conditions.

What do you want to do this cycle?

Consider which goals will move you forward during this cycle. It may be the six new ideas you listed. It could be a previous initiative or idea. There's no wrong answer. You can discuss several scenarios with your PACE team to choose which specific goals to choose.

Make sure you keep the evidence you identified in mind while you do this. The data you have about an idea can help you to prioritize which one is most likely to work right now.

Set a relative priority for each goal.

You will make weekly decisions about tasks when you execute the plan. Which tasks you choose will depend on the relative priority of your goals. So you need a way to prioritze.

For each goal set a relaive priority level. Look at how each goal relates to the other goals you've chosen for this cycle only. Not overal, just for this cycle. This will help you figure out which goals to work on first in the next step. That helps you manage resources more effectively.

As you go through successive PACE cycles the relative priority of projects will change. That's why we don't give the goal an "overall" priority, only a priority for the cycle. The website project may be high priority this month, but as it progresses those tasks may be less important each week. The major tasks give you a working site. Minor improvements may be able to wait until later. Another goal may also become critical as things change each week. The relative goal priority also gives you flexibility to shift actions to match shifting priorities as you need.

Make a note of why you chose these goals at this time.

Jotting down the purpose for this goal for this cycle can help you choose tasks each week. When things change you can re-evaluate if a particular set of tasks is still valid or not.

You may shift goal priorities as conditions change. One goal may becomes less, or more, relevant during the cycle. If you need to change direction or focus on another areas you can. The entire PACE structure is designed to be flexible so you can adjust on the fly.

CREATE

GOALS FOR THIS CYCLE

DATE _____

PRIMARY GOAL	PRIORITY	PURPOSE

Above is a form you can use for this exercise. If you have the capability, you can print it and fill it in by hand. You can also just draw your own on a sheet of paper, notebook, on a flip chart, or a whiteboard if you'd prefer. Then you can fill in the information for each cycle as you see fit.

Visit www.reinventingyourbusiness.net to see what on-line or downloadable tools as we develop them. They are not required but you may find them valuable. Full disclosure; supplemental tools may be at additional cost.

Everyday Tasks

In this exercise you'll capture major daily, weekly and miscellaneous tasks that need to be done during this cycle. The Activities Checkup can help identify things to consider for this step.

Running a business is full of normal, repetitive tasks. This is helpful in making sure you plan enough time to accomplish your new ideas and still perform normal functions. Many goals fail because we don't fully consider the time required and create unrealistic demands on our time. This activity makes sure you don't fall into that trap. Capture enough detail so you don't forget to leave time to do payroll, get deposits to the bank, or create the staff schedule, but don't go crazy.

ACTIVITIES CHECKUP	
How are you delivering to clients now?	How are you keeping in touch with customers now?
What activities are you focusing on now?	What are the three biggest challenges you face?

All tasks take up time.

It's important that you identify these tasks now because later you will be focused on doing tasks. Many of us forget to plan for routine tasks when setting goals. If you spend all your time on those, you won't be able to work on your new ideas.

By making sure your regular day-to-day activities are accounted for, you will be better able to evaluate which of your new ideas or experiments you can actually achieve each week.

Making a concious choice about what to attempt each week also help you stay focused and give you momentum. Raction mode is useful, but it can be demotivating. When you are choosing with purpose, instead of just reacting to things every week you're more likely to make progress with more confidence. That creates a sense of motion that can also help everyone's attitude. Business owners are wired to act. When we see a threat we respond from our core programming. Perceived threats trigger our "fight or flight" response. That's normal, but if it goes on for too long it can lead to frantic activity... just trying stuff to be doing anything.

Stress can help, or it can hinder.

When you're in a high stress state activity can feel good. It releases chemicals to reduce immediate stress. Thinking "I'm doing something" also gives you a sense of control. If the threat doesn't go away, however, the anxiety will creep back in. That can make things worse in the long run. Activity feels good now, but it may not be helpful if that activity isn't making a dent in the problem causing the stress in the first place.

There are other ways to release pent up stress. Exercise, eating well, and sleep are the easiest. Those can help you think with a clear head when deciding what actions are best for business.

CREATE

REGULAR OPERATIONAL TASKS

DAILY	WEEKLY	MISC

Above is a form you can use for this exercise. If you have the capability, you can print it and fill it in by hand. You can also just draw your own on a sheet of paper, notebook, on a flip chart, or a whiteboard if you'd prefer. Then you can fill in the information for each cycle as you see fit.

Visit www.reinventingyourbusiness.net to see what on-line or downloadable tools as we develop them. They are not required but you may find them valuable. Full disclosure; supplemental tools may be at additional cost.

CREATE

Your List of Tasks

Now have your PACE team study the two task lists you've created. It's time to identify the list of tasks that you want to work on during this particular PACE cycle. Start with your goal tasks, then add your every day tasks. List all the TASKS you think you'll be able to tackle in the time you've chosen for the cycle (30 or 60 days usually). This can take a bit of time, and it may seem monotonous, but it is where you will pick all your tasks for the next month or two for this process. These tasks are the ones you feel are important and that you want to get done now.

GOALS FOR THIS CYCLE		DATE
PRIMARY GOAL	PRIORITY	PURPOSE

Create a Backlog list.

To create your Backlog you can copy the sheet on the next page, use a whiteboard, or a flipchart if you'd prefer. On it list all the tasks you identified. You may need more than one piece of paper if your list is long.

It's important to list the tasks, not the goals or milestones. The tasks are the things you will actually "do" each week.

You may end up working on tasks from several goals, or just one at a time. That's up to you. If you're not working on a goal right now don't include those goal tasks in this backlog. You may revisit them for a future PACE cycle.

These should be tasks you feel will have high impact. Don't worry about getting it exactly right. You'll get better at this process as you go through successive cycles.

Prioritize your Backlog items.

Then set a relative priority for each. Simple ratings are best (1/2/3, etc.). This is their priority for this PACE cycle. Focus on the tasks that are most meaningful and productive right now.

Assign the task to someone.

Identify who will be responsible for managing each task. That may be the person who actually does the work or whoever is responsible for overseeing that it gets done, like a manager. Try not to overload a single person too much, including yourself.

Be as realistic as you can about how much each person can do. Your goal is to complete each task in one week or less, if possible. Don't just pile things on. That's also why we include operational tasks. Be as realistic as you can with resource managment each week.

CREATE

TASK BACKLOG THIS CYCLE

DATE

TASK	PRIORITY	ASSIGNED	TASK	PRIORITY	ASSIGNED

Above is a form you can use for this exercise. If you have the capability, you can print it and fill it in by hand. You can also just draw your own on a sheet of paper, notebook, on a flip chart, or a whiteboard if you'd prefer. Then you can fill in the information for each cycle as you see fit.

Visit www.reinventingyourbusiness.net to see what on-line or downloadable tools as we develop them. They are not required but you may find them valuable. Full disclosure; supplemental tools may be at additional cost.

STEP 4:
EXECUTE
YOUR PLAN

EXECUTE

In This Section...

It's time to start taking action! You've defined the tasks you want to accomplish now you'll use a very specific project management format, called a SPRINT, to start working on them. If you are familiar with the SPRINT, notice I'm suggesting a length of one week. That's to help line up with the calendar most businesses already use as a 'cycle' and to simplify the process. Variable lengths are possible, but I recommend keeping things as simple as possible. Each week you will choose tasks to tackle that week, then you'll get to work. You'll track progress as you go.

Stay focused on the tasks at hand.

Be careful not to get distracted by other things that come up in the middle of your week. If you and your PACE team have been thoughtful about choosing tasks each week, those tasks should drive your priorities. Unless something major changes, stay on track and focus on getting those tasks done. It will also give you more confidence and help minimize distraction or confusion.

Time: 1 hour/week, 15 min/day (average)

The process will be ongoing through the cycle (30 or 60 days as you've chosen). You'll set up a new SPRINT each week. That should take an hour or less. Each day you'll review your progress for about 15 minutes. Your needs may vary. You will also get more efficient as you go along.

Here are the steps you'll be going through as you execute the plan:

Simplifying Agile Methodology

This section uses tools created to help developers and designers create innovative software and products. This process and methods may, or may not, be familiar to you. If it is, please keep in mind this is a very simplied adaptation of very complex methodologies. The goal is to make the process accessible to anyone, even if they aren't familiar with Agile, or project management as a practice. If you are an experienced Agile professional and you want to make that work to your advantage by all means do so. This is designed to be flexible.

If you are not familiar with Agile, or it's methods and tools, don't worry. You don't need to know anything more than I' will explain. I'll go over what you need to know and do in the next few pages. You may find it both a bit strange and yet familiar. Hang in there, you'll get it after you start using it. Once you're familiar with the process you can make adjustments as you like. I just recommend you not change too much right away. That will give you a chance to get a sense of how the whole process works. Then you can use the tools in any way that does your the most good. This is about you making progress. That's the most important thing here.

EXECUTE

Review Your Task Backlog

At the beginning of every SPRINT refer to the Backlog for tasks.

TASK BACKLOG THIS CYCLE

DATE _____

TASK	PRIORITY	ASSIGNED	TASK	PRIORITY	ASSIGNED

The SPRINT Board

All the action happens here each week to get things done one step at a time.

THE SPRINT BOARD

DATE _____

TO DO	IN PROGRESS	DONE

Running a SPRINT

Each week you will chose a list of tasks to try and complete that week. Yo will list them on your SPRINT board. You can copy the one in this book, create one on a whiteboard, flipchart or even use post it notes on a wall with three columns. It's up to you. The board tracks where you are with each task. You'll move them from "To Do", to "In Progress, to "Done" each week.

TO DO	IN PROGRESS	DONE
Create Facebook posts		
Set up sugar shipment		
Interview sales candidates		
Create schedule		
Interview top 3 customers		

Add the tasks you will attempt to "To Do"

TO DO	IN PROGRESS	DONE
Create Facebook posts		
	Set up sugar shipment	
Interview sales candidates		
	Create schedule	
Interview top 3 customers		

As you start tasks move them to "In Progress"

TO DO	IN PROGRESS	DONE
	Create Facebook posts	
		Set up sugar shipment
	Interview sales candidates	
		Create schedule
Interview top 3 customers		

As they are completed move them to "Done"

Choose a SPRINT Team

Each week pick a team of folks to help manage the SPRINT tasks. It can be your staff, partners or others. These folks could be doing activities, overseeing actions or just helping you keep track of your progress. The SPRINT team might change week to week, as needs shift.

Watch Out for Blocks

Sometimes you can't move a task forward because something prevents progress. When that happens work on the "block" instead. Your team should always be working to complete tasks OR to clear blocks so they CAN work on completing the tasks each week.

You are either clearing a block.   OR   *Working to complete a task.*

Daily Stand-ups

Each day you will check your progress to determine if any changes are needed and plan the day ahead. this is called your stand-up. It helps keep you on track every day of the week and allows you to make changes or adjustments in the tasks you're working on every day. If priorities change one week, you can change the plan for which tasks to add to the SPRINT next week. Maximum flexibility while still keeping the process simple and easy to understand is the key.

A Retrospective to Learn Lessons

At the end of the week you will review what was accomplished in the SPRINT and think about what you can do better then next week. We call this a "retrospective". How many tasks were you able to complete? Did you notice something that worked particularly well? Notice that so you can use it again. If you noticed that something else didn't work, make an adjustment.

Develop the team as you go.

You can make adjustment in your team between SPRINTs too. You may base the team on the tasks you've chosen for that week. Matching skills to actions. It's that kind of flexibility that makes the process so useful and powerful. It's not called Agile for nothing!

EXECUTE

Setting up a SPRINT

Executing your plan will consist of working to complete a list of tasks each week. Each week you will complete as much as you can. Each week you will note your progress, reset the SPRINT board and repeat the process the next week. This continues until the end of the cycle.

This succession of SPRINTs allows you to focus on a fixed set of tasks each week, choosing which priorities are most important now. This structure helps prevent distraction and allows you manage resources effectively. It also gives you a daily spot check, and a more in depth check-in point weekly, to make changes or adjustments as needed throughout the cycle.

Choosing tasks from your Backlog

The SPRINT starts by choosing a set of tasks you want to complete this week from your Backlog

Pick your most high priority goal tasks, then include operational tasks for that week. Each task should be able to be done in one week or less. If needed, you can carry an incomplete task over to another week, but the idea is to complete tasks whenever possible.

TASK BACKLOG THIS CYCLE						DATE
TASK	PRIORITY	ASSIGNED		TASK	PRIORITY	ASSIGNED

Put the tasks on the SPRINT Board

List all the tasks for that week in the "To Do" column. Everything you will attempt should be listed. You'll get better at 'sizing' as you do SPRINTS each week. Sizing is simply figuring out how many tasks you can really handle each week. Tasks require different time and effort. How many you can do will change based on how much effort each will take to complete.

The "To Do" Column

Don't worry about next week, focus on this week's tasks. Pick a task and get started on it. If you can start on more than one task at a time, then do so. It's just that simple. Go!

The "In Progress" Column.

As soon as you begin working on a task, move it to the next column. You can start multiple tasks as you need but don't move it until you actually start actually acting on it.

The "Done" Column.

When you've completed a task move it to the last column. Success! The goal each week is do this with as many tasks as you can, clearing the board as much as possible.

EXECUTE

THE SPRINT BOARD

DATE

TO DO	IN PROGRESS	DONE

Above is a form you can use for this exercise. If you have the capability, you can print it and fill it in by hand. You can also just draw your own on a sheet of paper, notebook, on a flip chart, or a whiteboard if you'd prefer. Then you can fill in the information for each cycle as you see fit.

Visit www.reinventingyourbusiness.net to see what on-line or downloadable tools as we develop them. They are not required but you may find them valuable. Full disclosure; supplemental tools may be at additional cost.

During the SPRINT

Be careful not to change too much unless it's critical! Chasing shiny objects can slow you down and defeat the purpose of the SPRINT. Focus on your priorities helps you maintain momentum.

Continue to work on as many tasks as you can through the week. It's okay that you don't complete them all. You'll get better at what can realistically get done each week fairly quickly.

Have a daily Stand-up meeting.

Every day take a look at what you did and what's left for the week. It can be at the end of the day or the beginning of the next, your choice. Take a few minutes (15 - 30 normally) and note the progress you made. Were there any issues? Did anything pop up to block progress? What did you learn that day? Did you complete any tasks? Celebrate those with the team.

Next, look at the next day. Decide where to focus. Do you need to make any adjustments? Any priority changes to make? What resources will you need to work on those tasks? Is there anyone that needs assistance? Do you need to call on your Key People or PACE team for help?

After the SPRINT evaluate the board and reset.

At the end of each SPRINT review the past week. How did you do? What did you finish and what was left over? Note how much you did vs what you attempted. Mark tasks in the "Done" column as completed in your task Backlog. Great job! Celebrate those wins with the team.

When that's done, clear the board of everything. Yes, even "In Progress" tasks. Each SPRINT starts with a clean board. Don't worry, you can put those tasks on next week or later.

Next, review your task Backlog. Choose a new set of tasks for next week based on your present situation and conditions. They might be new, they might be tasks you didn't finish from last week, or they might be the next task in a goal you're working on this cycle.

This new task list becomes your new SPRINT. If a task was "In Progress" previously you can move it to that column once you start working on it again. Don't move it before that though.

SPRINT to the end of your PACE cycle.

Remember, if you can't make progress on a task, focus on removing whatever is blocking it instead. Once the block is cleared, continue making progress on the task until it's done. You will continue to repeat this pattern, week after week, until the PACE cycle is complete.

You will complete SPRINTs each week back to back for the entire PACE cycle. Hopefully, you're making progress on your new idea goals. You'll take a look at what heppened each cycle too, so you can identify where things are going well and where you need to focus more effort.

EXECUTE

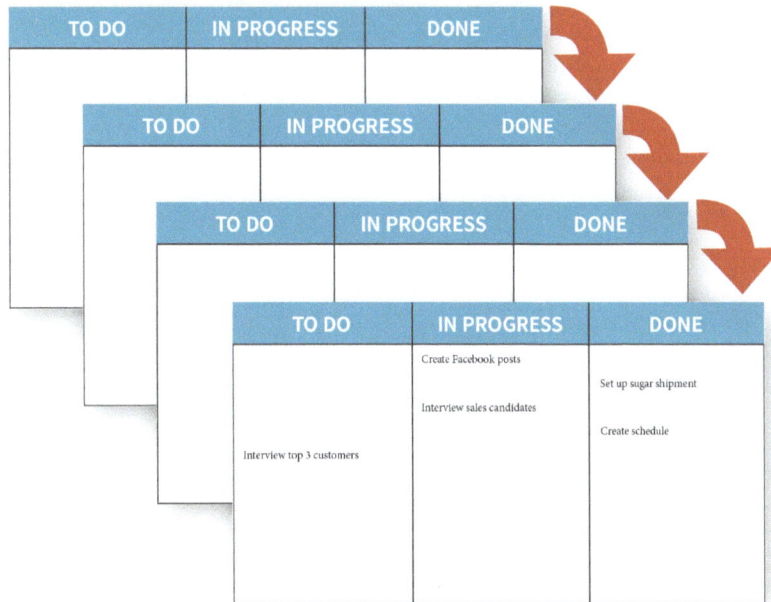

During each PACE cycle you will either run four SPRINTs (30 days) or eight SPRINTs (60 days)

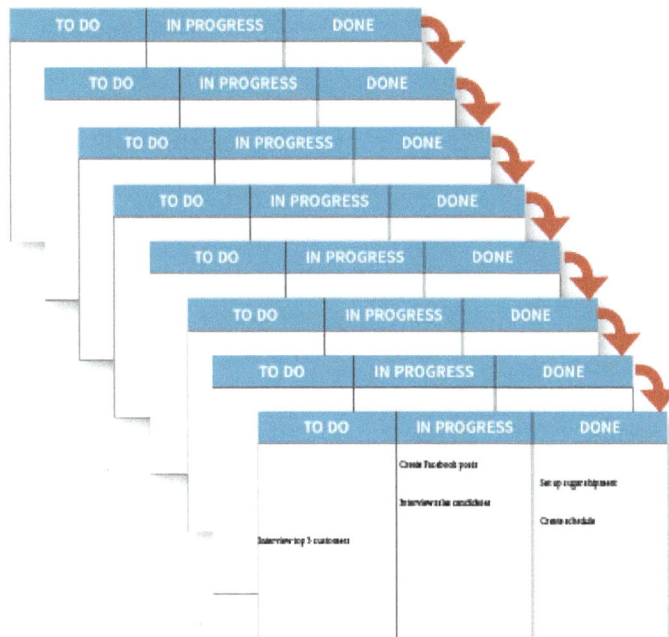

EXECUTE

Choosing SPRINT Tasks

Here are a couple of tips for picking the best tasks for your SPRINT each week.

Use your goal priorities as a guide. Work on higher priority tasks first. This should help you stay focused on things that have the biggest impact on your business at the beginning.

Resist distractions and stay focused.

You gave goals and tasks their priority for a reason. Use that to your advantage. You decided those tasks were important. Trust yourself. If you identified it as important why should something else side track you from that task or goal? Use that to help manage distractions and keep you focused. Only change a priority if something major changes.

TASK BACKLOG THIS CYCLE					
TASK	PRIORITY	ASSIGNED	TASK	PRIORITY	ASSIGNED

There are always distractions. Only change your focus if something of greater value or priority presents itself. Otherwise, stay on course. People will ask you to do other things. Opportunities will pop up. They may seem urgent. They may look good. Try not to get side tracked. There are lots of urgent things to steal your attention away from important ones. Getting distracted is the downfall of many projects and has hurt many small businesses.

Trust yourself and the process.

You can absolutely change direction if something really does need immediate attention. Just be careful of 'shiny object' syndrome. That distraction can cost you valuable time, energy and resources that are better spent focused on achieving your higher priority goals.

Under stress and anxiety we are all more likely to have doubts about what they're doing. This process helps you be more confident by reducing the feeling you have to react to everything immediately. It reduces your level of anxiety and panic.

Your choices will be based on evidence and thinkiing, not emotional reaction only. That won't make anxiety go completely, but it can help you trust yourself to clearly evaluate the things that do pop up, and help you avoid distracting side trips.

EXECUTE

If something happens mid-SPRINT.

It is possible that something noteworthy could happen in the middle of the week. You'll need to process it in your daily stand-up and decide how to react. You can always make adjustments to the SPRINT board as needed if something significant happens. You can make that call.

If may be less disruptive if you can wait until the end of the SPRINT to add those new tasks. Put them into the Backlog and pick up the following week. This will allow you to rethink your priorities too, taking account of new information or events. Then you can make adjustments as needed to address the situation on the ground having throught it all the way through.

If something major happens mid-PACE.

The same goes for the larger structure of a PACE cycle. If you're part way through a cycle and a major event or significant change occurs, just PAUSE and start a new PACE cycle at that point.

This ability to Plan/Execute/Adjust is what makes the PACE structure so useful for very short term planning. You retain control over your actions and how you decide to react to things that happen, even if you don't have control of your overall situation or the buisness environment.

Instead of being constantly buffeted by events with no idea what to do next, PACE allows you to get your bearings and set a direction at any point in time. Even in the middle of a PACE cycle itself. The reset button is always there if you need it. Pause, re-evaluate and re-plan.

PAUSE is there for a reason.

Unexpected things happen. Restarting a cycle is not failure, it is part of the process. It's what gives you ultimate flexibility to respond as you need in any situation.

That means your actions are always more purposeful and more likely to be productive in helping you sustain your business. That makes it easier to recover and rebuild towards profitability as soon as things are more stable and longer term planning is a viable option.

It helps you act with confidence because you will know what you're doing and why you're doing it at all times. Even if you end up not being correct all the time. You can always make adjustments to stay on a positive course no matter how external conditions change.

We all make mistakes, it's how you recover from those mistakes that determines how well your business does in the long run. Keep making adjustments as needed until things open up.

STEP 5:
PAUSE
AGAIN TO PLAN

After the last SPRINT

Once you've completed one full PACE cycle we need to PAUSE again. It's time to see what you've completed, re-evaluate where you are now, and determine what's going on with your business and the environment it lives in before you start another cycle.

Lessons Learned Exercise

Before we close this cycle out completely, make note of how this cycle went. You're going to be looking at what you did well, what you can improve, and what lessons you learned. I suggest looking at things honestly. These lessons can make future cycles work more smoothly and be more productive. You'll get better at the process the more you do this exercise.

What Did You Accomplish?

Make note of what you got done. Even if you didn't complete a goal, you want to track your progress. Note how much you attempted, and accomplished during each SPRINT. This will help you size future SPRINTs more accurately. Seeing that you can still take action and get things done can go a long way to restoring your confidence too.

What Did You Learn?

Was there anything that you know now that you didn't know when you started this cycle? These lessons can help you get better, faster and more efficient at the process. They also may hold the key to new ideas and experiments you can try in future cycles.

What Did You Do Well?

Take a bow! Acknowledge when you and the team shine. It can be a huge morale booster. This helps everyone stay motivated and on track when times are uncertain. Way to go.

What Can You Improve?

Did you notice some things you could do better? Be honest, but also forgiving. These lessons can make the next cycle even better. Can you commit to at least a little improvement every cycle? If so, you can see big results fast. Improvement compounds over time.

How well did the PACE team work?

It's also useful to note how well your PACE team functioned this cycle. Did you have the right people on the team? Did they work well together and with you? Were there any conflicts? Can you make additions or changes that would be useful next cycle?

Changing the team members is normal. If someone isn't clicking they can be a drag on the process. Your PACE team can help you find blind spots and think more creatively.

PAUSE

LESSONS LEARNED THIS CYCLE

DATE _____

WHAT WE ACCOMPLISHED	WHAT WE LEARNED	WHAT WE DID WELL	WHAT WE CAN IMPROVE

Above is a form you can use for this exercise. If you have the capability, you can print it and fill it in by hand. You can also just draw your own on a sheet of paper, notebook, on a flip chart, or a whiteboard if you'd prefer. Then you can fill in the information for each cycle as you see fit.

Visit www.reinventingyourbusiness.net to see what on-line or downloadable tools as we develop them. They are not required but you may find them valuable. Full disclosure; supplemental tools may be at additional cost.

Start a New PACE Cycle

Now it's time to go back to start the process again with a new PACE cycle. You'll repeat the steps starting with setting a new cycle length and start date. Then you select a PACE team for this cycle. It may be the same people, it may include some different folks this time around.

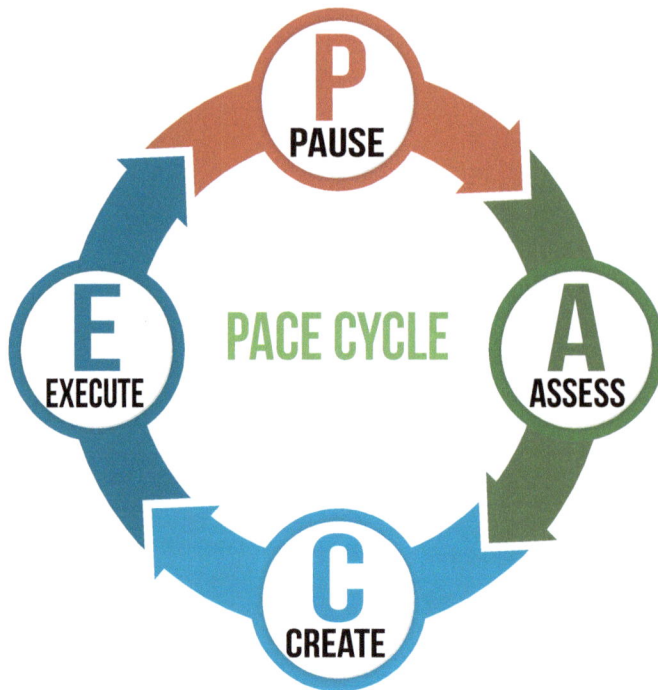

You'll repeat the ASSESS stage as you did before. This time may be easier since you already have the information from the last cycle as a starting point.

Then you'll CREATE a new list of goals and tasks. Confirm your operational tasks and create a new Backlog for this cycle.

Next you'll start running SPRINTs again, making adjustments as you go. Complete that PACE cycle and then you'll start over again. This can go on as long as you need, until there's stability.

Stay focused on your value to customers.

Every time you complete a cycle you'll get better at planning SPRINTs, and noticing where you are having an impact. You'll get faster and more efficient at responding to changes and anticipating what your clients value as you go. Don't lose sight of that.

Delivering value is the key to sustaining your business over time. Knowing what your customers value about what you offer means they buy. That may change over time. We expect that it will. Especially if you're running your business in the midst of a period of instability, like a pandemic.

As things fluctuate their behavior will fluctuate too. It turns out that buyer confidence during COVID is a critical issue. If people don't feel safe, they won't go out and buy. You need to pay attention to where they are and meet them there.

Your situation may change week to week or month to month, as customers perceptions change. The external environment is just one aspect of how your customers behave. Stay focused on what they see as valuable and how you can provide it. That is the key.

PACE is designed to be repeated.

PACE is designed to be flexible and repeatable. Once you get the process down, you can adjust each cycle length to match the situation. Determine what makes the most sense based on what's happening when you PAUSE at the end of one cycle and before you begin the next cycle.

The process gives you a repeatable process that can change as needed while keeping you pointed forward. It also keeps you from running too far ahead of events and getting lost or distracted by plans that are irrelevant by the time you execute them.

Use succesive PACE cycles for as long as you need, repeating cycles until you feel stable enough to plan out farther. Then you can switch to the business planning method you used before. Once things are more stable you can shift your focus to getting profitable again, not just sustaining or surviving the crisis period. Hopefully, it helps you recover more quickly too.

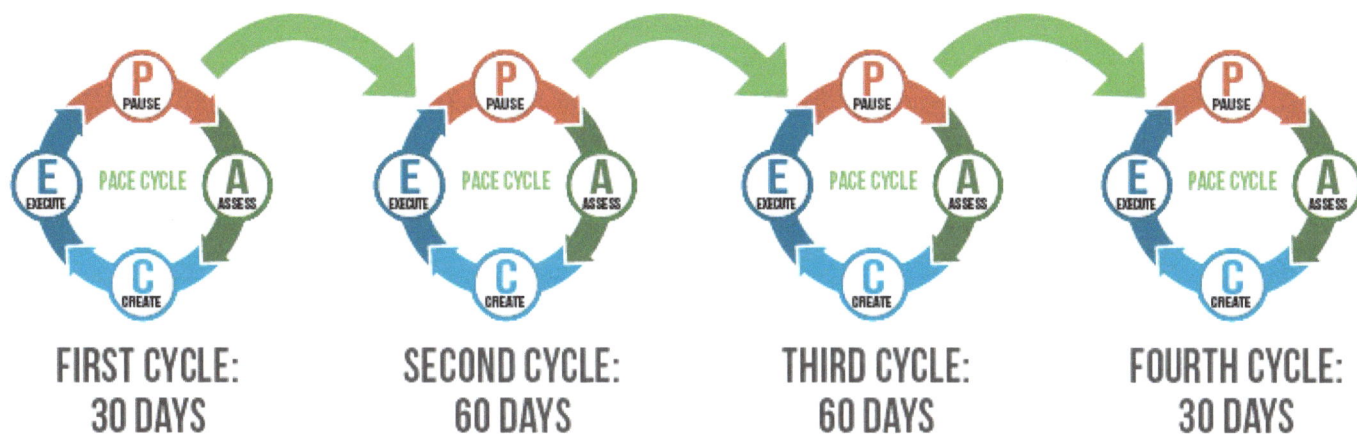

FIRST CYCLE: 30 DAYS   **SECOND CYCLE: 60 DAYS**   **THIRD CYCLE: 60 DAYS**   **FOURTH CYCLE: 30 DAYS**

Every repetition of the PACE cycle is an opportunity to make changes and re-evaluate your "plan".

As the situation changes, you can make adjustments based on your current business reality, based on how your customers are reacting, and what resources you have available.

NEXT STEPS: BEYOND THE PANDEMIC

Lessons from 2020

When this edition of the RYB Workbook is being released we are still in the midst of the COVID-19 pandemic. While that historic event was the genesis of this book the ideas are actually valid beyond any such time or economic event.

As I write this, we don't know how and when things will stabilize. It's the economic instability that makes this workbook important right now. It can help you survive and sustain as long as you need it. Keep working the process to brainstorm how to respond as long as necessary.

The tools in the workbook were chosen for that purpose. However, the underlying ideas behind those tools are true all the time. These concepts are fundamental to the success of your business no matter what the environment, in good times and in bad times.

Change is the only constant.

The first idea is innovation. If you allow complacency to sneak up on you, it can kill your business. What you did last year will not be exactly right for your business this year, or next year. During the pandemic we are just seeing change amplified and accelerated, compressed into weeks and months instead of years. It happens all the time, just more slowly.

In order to create a sustainable business you must be able to flex and adapt. This book helps make the process of change intentional. You decide how to change, on purpose. That ability to innovate and shift will help determine if you grow or stagnate. Adapt or die. Keep these tools handy, they can help you face change later too at any point in your journey.

Business is all about delivering value.

Two other concepts at the heart of this book are "value" and "perspective". Understanding your customer's perception of value is what matters most. It's easy to lose sight of that if you've had some success. Sure, you need to believe in what you do and have a passion for it, but if your customer doesn't see what you do as valuable he or she will not pay you money for it. Then things fall apart quickly. Avoiding the curse of knowledge and seeing things as they do is a skill that could make or break your business, even when the economy is good.

Business is ultimately a math problem. What makes that equation work is that you know who wants to buy and what value they get by buying from you. Deliver that value to them and they will consistently buy from you, driving revenue that keeps your business alive.

CUSTOMERS ACTUALLY BUY VALUE.

The Five Key Questions

I've helped hundreds of businesses create plans over the years. My experience is that most people hate writing a business plan. One day i realized what they hate is the document, not the idea of planning. A traditional business plan format is the same as a research paper. Ugh! No wonder people don't like writing those. Not everyone likes writing research papers.

Instead I recommend thinking about what's in the business plan, instead of the format of the document. I've been using the following five questions to help people create basic business plans for the last several years. The answers to these questions provide you most of the basic information you need to determine whether a business is likely to work. The answers to the questions become the plan. Much the way the goals and tasks in this Workbook became actions in your SPRINTs. Try it and see what you discover about your own business.

I refer to these questions as The Five Elements because they are the basic information you need to build a sustainable business. They are fundamental to your success. They are as follows:

- *What problem(s) am I trying to address in the market?*

- *Who has the problem(s) I'm offering to solve?*

- *What is my specific solution(s) to those problem(s) for those specific people?*

- *What resources do I need to create/deliver the solution(s)?*

- *What do I need to measure to determine if the plan is working?*

Questions are helpful. When you ask a question, your brain immediately tries to answer it. The more relevant and specific the question, the more useful the answer will be to you.

The answers to these five questions can be as simple or as detailed as you want. They can help you create a high level elevator pitch or define all the details to create a multi-page business plan document for a bank. It's up to you how you use it. I offer it here as a simpler way to think about how you plan for your business. Hopefully they will help simplify the process so you stay focused on what you're doing in your business, who you're doing it for, and why.

CUSTOMERS WILL ONLY PAY FOR WHAT THEY THINK IS VALUABLE.

Getting More Help

There are many resources available to help you run your business. Below are some publically funded programs that I highly recommend. They are all programs supported by tax dollars through the Small Business Administration. Use them, they provide no-cost and low cost services for any small business in all 50 states in the United States.

U.S. Small Business Administration (SBA):

www.sba.gov

Small Business Development Centers:

www.americassbdc.org

SCORE Association:

www.score.org

Reinventing Your Business Website:
www.reinventingyourbusiness.net

I put together a website that has both free and paid content that you may find useful. It will be clear which things cost money and which don't. I will also always let you know if I make money from somthing through an affiliate relationships (like books, classes, software, etc.).

What you will find:

- Supplemental Information Downloads
- Lists of Books and Other Resources
- Online Course Information (future)
- Coaching and Support Resources (future)
- "The Reinventing Your Business Podcast"

ACKNOWLEDGMENTS

No man (or woman) is an island.

This workbook is the culmination of many hours spent pondering, discussing and refining ideas. I would not have been able to pull it all together, especially as quickly as I did, without the patience, feedback, and, most importantly, time from some truly wonderful people. I appreciate them indulging me when I had a brainstorm, sharing ideas and giving me suggestions, or just letting me ramble on until I figured out how to make the blasted thing work. I could not have done it without each of them and I am eternally grateful for their support, encouragement, excitement and most of all for helping me get beyond just talking about it and actually writing it all down, finally.

Mary Noyce Joynt
Barbara Ann Beisler
Kimberly LaFave
John Binkley
Kate Janich
Amy Dagliano
Dan Hine
Subodh Nayar
Demetrios Sapounas
Cort Maddox

Thank you all for your help, feedback, support and inspiration. It means the world to me.

Who Is Eric L. Byrd?

Eric has been telling stories of one kind or another for over 30 years. As an editor, producer and writer in television after college, as a salesperson for over 20 years in the video technology and IT world and as a business trainer, then coach, since 2010.

Making a study of how people communicate is as much a passion as vocation for Eric. He loves to understand what makes things, and people, tick. He loves sharing information with others to help create light bulb moments of inspiration and understanding for his clients. Eric thinks you can learn volumes by asking a dumb question and encourages his clients to explore, stretch and expand their limits at ever opportunity.

In 2015 he began working full time as a small business coach in Northern Virginia. Since then he has coached hundreds of businesses, new and existing alike. He never tires of helping small business owners be more effective, more intentional, and to help them understand their customers better. He is always asking 'why' about everything.

In October 2019 he launched the Adventures in Networking podcast. A show focused on referral networking and building relationships in business. During the 2020 COVID-19 pandemic he launched the Reinventing Your Business podcast to inspire small businesses by sharing stories from others just like them.

Eric is frequently a speaker, sometimes an author and always a proud father and grandfather. His favorite activity is being silly for no reason with his grandson, Mason, while they have wild and wonderful adventures at his home in Leesburg, Virginia.

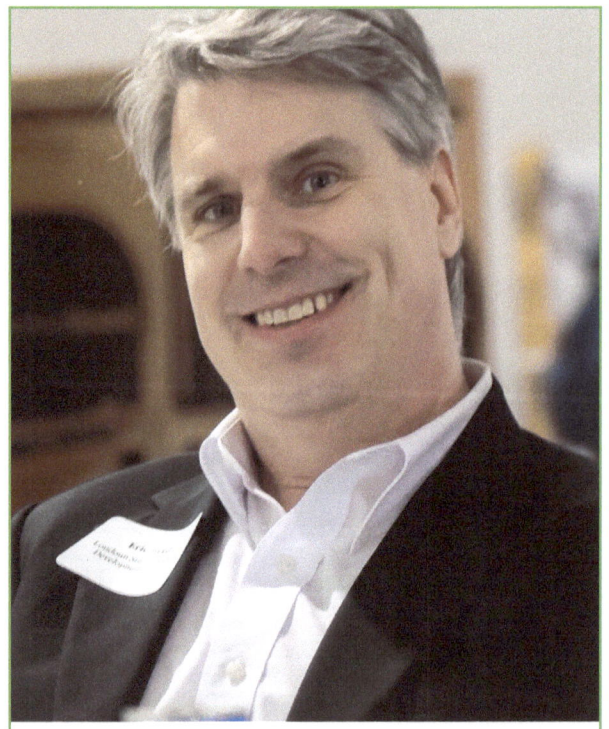

Photo by Mason Baker

For more information visit *www.reinventingyourbusiness.net*